# Schnauzer

## Pet journal and record keeper to record your dog's life as it happens!

# Introduction

This Schnauzer journal and record keeper preserves the precious moments!

There is lots of space for snapshots of your best friend and companion! This blank book gives dog lovers the opportunity to chart their puppies growth.

As your puppy grows into an adult you can document and capture the cherished moments.

There is a page for birth information, vaccine records, and even a page to place your puppy's paw prints!

You can take photos of your puppy discovering his world as he grows into an adult. This blank book is the ultimate keepsake for every dog owner!

There are pages that allow you to add a photo then write what your puppy or dog did that day.

Don't miss the happy moments when your companion is sleeping, bounding across the yard, his first birthday or his favorite things to do!

With this dog memory book you will be able to admire and preserve your favorite memories to enjoy the happy moments for years!

Start creating lasting memories today with this journal and scrapbook for your puppy or dog!

*A dog is the only thing on earth that loves*
*you more than you love yourself.*
*~Josh Billings*


*A dog will teach you unconditional love.*
*If you can have that in your life, things won't be too bad.*
*~Robert Wagner*

# My Schnauzer

Date of Birth: _____

Place of Birth: _____

Registered Name: _____

Call Name: _____

Father's Name: _____

Mother's Name: _____

# Puppy Paw Print

# Adult Paw Print

# Vaccination Records

| Age | Shot Date | Distemper | Parvo | Rabies | Deworm |
|---|---|---|---|---|---|
| 6 wks | | | | | |
| 10 wks | | | | | |
| 14 wks | | | | | |
| 1 Year | | | | | |
| 2 Year | | | | | |
| 3 Year | | | | | |
| 4 Year | | | | | |
| 5 Year | | | | | |
| 6 Year | | | | | |
| 7 Year | | | | | |
| 8 Year | | | | | |
| 9 Year | | | | | |
| 10 Year | | | | | |
| 11 Year | | | | | |
| 12 Year | | | | | |

Additional Medical:

Heartworm Testing:

1 Year____  2 Year____  3 Year ____  4 Year____ 5 Year____

6 Year____  7 Year____  8 Year ____  9 Year____ 10 Year____

# Vaccination Notes:

_____

_____

# Medical Record Notes:

_____

_____

_____

_____

_____

_____

_____

_____

_____

_____

# Medical Emergencies

# Memories

Don't miss the happy moments!

Start creating lasting memories today!

Photo Here

Photo Here

# Memories:

Photo Here

Photo Here

Memories:

Photo Here

Photo Here

# Memories:

Photo Here

Photo Here

# Memories:

Photo Here

Photo Here

Memories:

Photo Here

Photo Here

Memories:

Photo Here

Photo Here

## Memories:

Photo Here

Photo Here

# Memories:

Photo Here

Photo Here

Memories:

Photo Here

Photo Here

# Memories:

Photo Here

Photo Here

Memories:

Photo Here

Photo Here

# Memories:

Photo Here

Photo Here

# Memories:

Photo Here

Photo Here

# Memories:

Photo Here

Photo Here

# Memories:

Photo Here

Photo Here

Memories:

Photo Here

Photo Here

# Memories:

Photo Here

Photo Here

Memories:

_____

_____

_____

_____

_____

_____

_____

_____

_____

Photo Here

Photo Here

Memories:

Photo Here

Photo Here

Memories:

_____

_____

_____

_____

_____

_____

_____

_____

_____

Photo Here

Photo Here

# Memories:

Photo Here

Photo Here

Memories:

Photo Here

Photo Here

# Memories:

Photo Here

Photo Here

# Memories:

Photo Here

Photo Here

# Memories:

Printed in Great Britain
by Amazon